Strange Trades

KRISTY ODELIUS

Strange Trades

Shearsman Books
Exeter

Published in the United Kingdom in 2008 by
Shearsman Books Ltd
58 Velwell Road
Exeter EX4 4LD

www.shearsman.com

ISBN 978-1-905700-84-4

Acknowledgements:
Some of the poems in this collection have been published by the following,
to whose editors and publishers I am most grateful:
ACM: 'Ineffable Green Thing, Loved By All'; 'My Mister's Eyes Are Something
Like Dim Sum'; *Blue Sky Review:* 'Pantoum'; *Chicago Review:* 'Dress-up';
'Interview'; 'It's Curtains, ars poetica'; 'Thoughts of Falling, Pollen, Pare';
Combo: 'And How'; 'Three Flights in a Multiplying Sky'; *Eratio:* 'Slide'; *Diagram:*
'Impostor With Housemaid's Knee'; *Keep Going:* 'Baby, What Kind of Help
Do You Really Want?'; *La Petite Zine:* 'Dislocations Lessons'; *Locus Point:*
'Aubade, Big Eyes'; 'Ekphrastic'; 'Infestation By Islands'; 'Page. Pact. Buoy.
Body.'; *Moria:* 'Cardio/sky'; 'The Newlyweds Climb a Fence'; 'Nascent, Sage,
Gulfs of Air'; *Notre Dame Review:* 'Forecast'; *Pavement Saw:* 'The Atmosphere
Leaks a Troubadour'; *PFS Post:* 'The Virgins of Chicago (4)'; 'The Virgins of
Chicago (5)'; 'Equivalents'; *Seven Corners:* 'A Breath Catalogue'; 'No Breath
Found'; 'The Virgins of Chicago (3)'; *Sidereality:* 'Vertigo to Eros'; 'Raving
Stark Mad'; *Spiral Bridge:* 'We Make Strange Trades'; *Words on Walls:* 'Third
Grade'; 'Winter'.

'The Virgins of Chicago (3),' 'Thoughts of Falling, Pollen, Pare' and 'Cardio/
sky' have been reprinted in *The City Visible: Chicago Poetry for the New Century*
(Cracked Slab Books, 2007). 'The Virgins of Chicago (2)' was produced as a
broadside for the Poetry Center of Chicago and 'If We'd Met In The Swamp
It Would've Been Different' appeared on the Poetry Center of Chicago's
website, in conjunction with their 10th Annual Juried Reading selected by
Campbell McGrath (February 2005). Many of the poems appeared in the
chapbook *Bee Spit*, published by Dancing Girl Press, December 2007. Thanks
to publisher Kristy Bowen.

Cover image: detail from *Descent* by Kelly VanderBrug.

For my parents, with gratitude

Contents

I.

II.

Perhaps we ought to feel with more imagination.
                         —John Ashbery

I have thus endeavored to preserve the truth of the elementary principles of human nature, while I have not scrupled to innovate upon their combinations.
                         —Mary Shelley

I

Thoughts of Falling, Pollen, Pare

When champion-bred
leaves lie splayed
like minimum wage
sin, when sleep,
a raincoat czar,
spreads its liquid
hands thin, I'll say
   not on: *your life, your daddy's knee, a new knife blade.*

Try, swim the brackish margin
between holy and hole, the ocean's
backstitched locomotion loosely
recites "no, there's no such
night in prosaic blood" nodding
its great nose toward the
mollusky dance-floor.

When honey leaks from
eyes bent to breezes
eyes like peach pits
fragrant and useless,

the czar disappears into
the rain's rumpled plumage
my heart's gong-bruised knees
buckling through branches.

It's bee-spit
that blows me
   I admit
and you
away.

FORECAST

The wife is in the grip of being.
                    Anne Carson

                    ★

All around me orchestra
was spinning out algebra.

I said *closed*—
but eyelids hum,
recurring there.

A fan unfolding
you, sketching
clean birds
on my gold-brown thighs.

            I alleged,
            I am my love.

                    ★

I alleged pleasure
breakwater,
a violet storm.

Bare knees on a girl's rum sheets
burned a steel distance in me.

Two-tongue. Sea-eyed.
Sweet fuck thinking
my pink dresses
away to real seas.

I won't, but bear harder.

*

Curled in
a star's mouth,
black.

Warm as sick cats,
and bright.

When I say *now*
bite straight down.

*

Sponge-flowers
drift in
lullaby chambers,

a view of lime seeds.

Cut a window in my palm
sometimes to feel you.

I heard—*a lucky girl.*

Wrung like a hand waking to rainwater.

★

Morning flew down the beach,
loose cash, the wing
we stash keeps a ruby fog.

Each root lodged in
your beautiful used-to—
dawn, my green glass,
what I can't do with you.

"It's curtains, *ARS POETICA*"

Is this why I stand at my oeil-de-boeuf,
blowing sugar bubbles at that guy
in the snazzy black hood?

Nipples and waffles rustle
a mean last week, ruffle

the constellations oar-locked
along our shower curtain.

A falling,
my heart,
a crocus
stalls at dawn.

Street noise adjusts
its head, tumbled
among the oak leaves.

At home in the bushes, thimble-
berries fill, advance a plump sortie.

O thermostat!
Preside like a priest
over our mouths,
dreaming.

Somewhere, an offhanded window
winks from a sea-drowned cabin.

On the dock, faded gray paint
suggests "submerged rock."

Underwater, you there, you hear?

IF WE'D MET IN THE SWAMP,
IT WOULD'VE BEEN DIFFERENT

Our black eyes transparent, our home base a high
bat's nest stuffed in the chest of an arthritic cypress

named for a one-eyed chief, and several of his
descendents. Flowering water is the muck

of our breakfasts. We ease ourselves, we slip
into a sweet, a mosquito bath drawn from waters

we don't dare drain. Oh man, I don't like
the sound of that thunder. Gator jaws

are beautiful, like a gum-tree raft.
What is "natural"? What is "good" in a forest,

tucked under water? Cypress knees rise up from nowhere,
on fire, the light making coals of a root's reflection.

What is all this nonsense? We have swamps
on our conscience, like a lie that returns to

the edge of our dreams, laughing much louder
than our swimming fists. We are caught in a swamp

storm, out on the boardwalk, the sky falls toward
us with each cracking branch. The cypresses have

lived here so long in this silent buzz, they talk
of our dumb luck, they make us feel good,

as if we were already the past.

THREE FLIGHTS IN A MULTIPLYING SKY

Drawn to the door, she's
the Empress of More.

Climbing the stairs, he's
a rare emporium. Interlunar,

invisible, she scales the locked
doorway, works the oak floors.

Slide-rule star, he pauses
and climbs, a dissonant chime

asks "when to remember?"
In diminishing light, ornithic

November, she recalls a
configuration of seagulls.

Inclined towards the door,
reclusive carousel, her divided

mind roosts a drowned daffodil.
He ascends, considering "what

to forget." Is she the cursed bride,
the saluki's tooth, hunting dog

combed silky smooth? The key in
the lock, she falls to the door, over

the threshold his soft mouth
moves, salt marsh wet, a descant

of dread and scattered roots.

Aubade, Big Eyes

This morning everything's possible here.

> "In the church parking lot, stealth lovers part at dawn,
> making out in the spot marked *Reserved For Priest*.
> Stash the cold breakfast, I'll mend the sheets . . . With
> my animé hair, record your brilliant bones in cases of
> Chambord, Saki, beer chasers."

Eye of morning? Visual memory, mist.
Bathwater fills cuts on my fingers and gums.

Watching you smoke, like mathematics etched in orchid stems.
Give me a maulstick to steady my hand. Your eyes river-bed, or
Japanese green? Impish gaze auditioning the sky's faint a.m.
scrawl.

> Later, reticent and shuffling, I dream of being
> "liminal," or Coco Chanel who glamorously died
> the year I was born, confirming my post-apocalyptic
> existence.

Daybreak, reading Greek icons again.

St. Peter rimmed in pearls or accented with touches of ochre.
The women regret their dangling maturity, eyes resting sacred
against profane.

> Beguiling honeycomb riddled by bee moths, I like
waiting here for the light to change.

VERTIGO TO EROS

Turn back the white distance O nervous
maps! A sudden figure etched in the retina:

fitful angel snipping sutures, stitching
bizzaro costumes, near-sighted finery sways

the eye's mind, pendant on a chain.
Deft skeleton, such cargo—flesh,

my friend, brain's machinery going everywhere.
A fresh-washed face: elegy for the living—heavy

furrows weave the landscape. O my el greco!
skein of sad fictions, afflictions like bees

to a bright aster bed. On this island, failing eyesight
undresses the sea. Broken light narrows, pinpoints

barebosom working out tensions strung between
birdbones. Daily renaissance, brush-strokes

distorted by the glass, schoolchildren's eyes
turn on a dime, imprint the world. Your own

peculiar surface elongated, pressed
to crevices, cloud formations.

PANTOUM

for Michael and Joanne Anania

There, a red tempest
swims above the mountain rain.
The sea winds down.
Hibiscus, like clouds,

swims above the mountain. Rain:
petals counting a bright descent.
Hibiscus-like clouds—
red cactus-flower

petals. Counting a bright descent,
Campari and soda drifting
red. Cactus flower,
olives, potatoes—on the porch,

Campari and soda. Drifting,
Carmella calls to us:
olives! potatoes on the porch!
Vesuvius in plain view,

Carmella calls. To us,
everything unwinds, becomes
Vesuvius. In plain view,
a lemon rind is

everything. Unwinds. Becomes
dull. To the sea,
a lemon rind is
anything but

dull. To the sea!
There, a red tempest,
anything but
the sea, winds down.

EQUIVALENTS

1.
We knew, and it
always feels good
to know something.

We could die—a silver
laugh, a photograph, or
at the end of your knee.

2.
They said there's
a resemblance, clouds
in the freeze, a force
in our boots.

What I saw—something else,
your blue reaching back
like remembered grass

eyes filling slow with
the weight of ice.

On the porch love
is implicitly forged.
Today, to mimic its
drift is to see.

3.
It was moving the whole time,
as if to hold you from the light.

I held your head
in the snow as if
to tell you a form.

4.
Five fingers, how do they
glow? Sick like honey
in the scientific field—
your hand, and what it knows.

VI SES, WATER WORLD

Tuesday split our town on the orange
line. I dipped, blue crushed velvet pants
in mind, a rumbling truck
moving through the green eye,
reversing a night-light distance.

Like folding jeans, Jönköping, I crease the map on this city.

A spray of Danish crowns and city
busses, useless. Jangling pants.
On the back pockets tiny orange
meteors like cheap leeches. Distance
closes on cheeses, evening, eye-
lashes bracing white sugar-truck

clouds. We volumize, rewind, chilly truck
and wind behind us, cool eyes
lying back in air-conditioned pants.
Sweaty dashboard. Like an orange
determined to rock on this city,
your name is a loop for distance.

As if calculating each distance
between us—kilometers, centimeters, eye-
lets in time—might fabricate a new city.
Finer skin flung from the roof of an armored truck.
Discarded, sweet-tucked like tangled pants,
the last time an orange

fleece flushed your ragged head—orange
plant-planet, a carnival city
in which there is no sign for distance.

In a dream I gave you the slip at a truck
stop, slurping black coffee. Eye
candy strutted by in skinny pants

you'd never wear. All the smarty pants
in London couldn't purchase the distance
laking the lies of that finger-tip city.
Loosing the town on a fire truck,
raising the speed of orange,
riding water-spooled vowels in your eyes.

The lazy eye of City Terminal
in the distance. Against the orange
salt truck, our pants almost look clean.

BABY, WHAT KIND OF HELP DO YOU REALLY WANT?

Pleasure can be expressed in words, bliss cannot.
                                        Roland Barthes

It's a question for a tailor,
a kerosene lip, outlined
fibrous branches fit
to the sky's white lung.

[Brisk.] On the train
a listing agent
negotiates a closing.
Lake View Art Supply
desires the lost city,
organizing phantoms
over the rough street.

How satisfying to dream of
floating, at any moment to find
his long eyes, the drifting
hood of a green aubade.

You indicate habits, prettier
drafts. Check them against
the bells of this business,
the specific "if" pinpointing
order. Think carefully:

not the familiar hand
itself, but the outline
of the familiar hand
rests on your head.

It's warm and its weight is surprising.
You recall you wanted fire, a tutor.

Wait. The so-far text
is grand, is next, rising
out of history like a scandal,
a suggestion, a wet necklace.

The Atmosphere Leaks a Troubadour

Your body is a tropopause,

strophic, sunk. A tropical storm

reading the almanac of outlaws, or

your body. Is a tropopause

a celestial sump, slow clause

loosening east from my forearm?

Yours? Body is a trope, a pause.

Stroppy, sunk, a topical strum—

Reverie, or war

Gusts of gone scatter on the screen before dawn.

She breathes to batten down the credits of a blue midwinter
    dream.

Flutter-bap! is her keystroke, her beat, her self-design.

Morning is like that, only you don't know what's coming.
Later, the casement sings its branchy overture. The opera begins.
What mournful fairy follows, counting rooftops, accumulating
    their devotions?
Water-color bridge. A weather report. Two red socks half-buried
    in mud.
What stalks them down the street at dusk, and long before?
Flutter-bap is the rhythm of rust and wing, shuffle in the
    underbrush, yellow flame.
She vowed to crack down or let it go, to cinch it with steel drums,
    to spread it thin.
She decided to steal the finch's flutter.

DRESS-UP

The walk-in beckons moony and sass,
make-out light quivers oblique in a far

corner, all mornings sleep akimbo in this
albescent night, unhook the bloodroot

view, oozing. Some stalky femme cantilevers
out a second story window—it's true

we're supported only at one end, the other,
"oceanic ego" beneath a nimble cover.

Our sly demons are breakfast for two
hands. "O legs!" betrayed by panicked weavers

a longish swim might end in flood-loot.
What can't be put to some advantage lists,

a familiar *cantus firmus*. Breathing grist, brain ajar,
somewhere a plush partita commends a well-deserving ass.

Impostor With Housemaid's Knee

Briefly she sees "life is terrible."

Looking out she wants the window to be

lyrical about snow, dreamy for Hitchcock,

cold cash, hot property, anything.

But, it's "wet and cold with instrumentation."

Fountains tinkle in the distance.

She might say something

like "then, the thaw."

The smell of warm butter,

seven dollars, purple velour.

Wonderful dream!

This darkness is an apiary.

She risks saying—

her melancholy, *la finestra*,

moth's wing or transparent sting.

INTERVIEW

Misfire or surprise leaks
nimble lies. They do
it all in their tortoise
cells. They drive a jeep,
or recongeal. Jell-O mold,
mind-muffed, life-jackets
tucked around our
trembling blue medals.

The wind kicks, reminds me
of something unsettling,
the Mediterranean fruit fly,
how it's larvae swarm hot
on lemons and oranges.
However it feels, we're
baking a meditation, we're
moating the narrowbodied
Orphic crumbs. In your
brain's cheap all-night
diner, aren't you flying?
Sporting your rare parure?

Tell me I'm sutured, curled
up in the right angles of,
the propositions of, the riptide
of my pimp pas de trois.

II

Dislocation Lesson III

Kate and Adrian enter
like Hedda Gabler
and the real inspector
hound. The room is a dry
and third-term pregnancy.
The "daughters of albion"
refuse to leave though
their lamentations fall
in vain on glittering
multiply pierced ears.

I am my sweet red ring.
I am my mother's cystitis.
I am hanging from the oak
tree window, the very small
boy I used to be looking in.

Faces like thumbnails
dream of text messages.
It's late morning.
Sometimes there is sun.
Today there's a note
in my cerulean pocket.
It says heartbreak.

THE VIRGINS OF CHICAGO (1)

"The virgins of Chicago

must be getting somewhere,"
I mumble in the contraceptive
sun. The redheads dream of being
inhabited by bungalows, dusk
penetrates them, and it's almost as good.

Around two on the porch—child,
you wake up. Like stamps of the Madonna,
a lampshade covered in postage:
this is oddly reassuring and ugly.

AND HOW

How do we talk about this?
My sisters appear, three rings
of blue fire, "like cats coming
out of clocks." We left hours ago.
Left years. Once we were never
here in a room of mirrors, brief
slips of arm and teeth reflected
in our absences, echoes winding
from "planter of gardenias"
and "juicer" and "Turtle Wax."

Winter minds reach for something, lathe
snowflakes out of early visions. Scuffed
intricacies get scarfed, brain sliding one stem
to the next. Whose mouth, bright red
in the snow, knows whether or not
it lies beneath "the live?"

THE VIRGINS OF CHICAGO (2)

The virgins of Chicago
know why they despise vibrato.
Hovering suddenly above the alley,
into the open dumpster they fly
sucking Slurpees singing "I lick
the wind's behind." If only I could
inhale their sticky tongues, let go
"The Poet," the mellifluous throat
of aluminum desire, from jaws and
wallets draw Desnos, or daybreak's
nervous rotating dimes. *I summon*
to me tornadoes and hurricanes.
I give them household names. Outside,
chariots swing low in the neighbor's
mailbox. It's the singing I fear,
I'm not afraid of the song.

Novatrix

after Ashbery

The girl behind the yellow fan
and the city cop, they were here?
The desk, leaning to light—
is it here, too?
Or none—the small hurts,
her footprints on the window,
the cuffs of fat, eastern winter?

The cop drops charges
in plain view, on the desk
lovely rings have long sunk out of sight.
Beneath her fringed hem the lies go dead.
Wings of fans keep them, but mute—liberation.

ELEGY

And so, moon-headed ship-man,
we came to a consensus.
A sailing, or a salting? Bring it
upstairs and dress it in mustard
seed distance. Scalloped and
horizontal day, blinking
sprints your wing, your
orange piece-meal skin.

This body has been here for many years.

In years, I'm making an eye
of an old song. Numbers in
love with perpendicular towers,
imperceptible falcons.
There's no herd of gold
rolling in tonight.

You, and a magnet.
You, and a red song.

The vowels in your fingernails
cross a long channel.
Did you see her, the girl
with the yellow leash?
A broken apple for heat.
Slow, or breathing.

THE NEWLYWEDS CLIMB A FENCE

After the light and the chandelier scraping,
the double-star making, it's hard to face
the red carpet, the casuistry show,

the vacuuming and dusting, the unquiet eye.
Do I wish I could give you "a bath of gold apples"
or "all the songs that sleep in history?" Maybe

this slant alternative is better—plucking lashes
from a winter magazine, little Domestic
winks, if we want, like Italian frames.

Night boats might ferry us further my friend.
Between our ribs, negatives of future architectures,
textures mind-nestled in flesh splinter-tender.

Let the bog-dwellers dream of American cars,
however grateful for "the Woman and the Dog."
We praise them all and drink our grape juices.

THE VIRGINS OF CHICAGO (3)

The virgins of Chicago

work nights at "Federal Screw
Products." They like welding,
sweating and wearing
gray aprons.

"I can't feel anything,"
I sigh as the elevator rises.
The meta-galaxy slips
like a ring on my finger,
a parenthesis squeezing the night
in towards morning.

They rest in the caliper,
thinking about tree
trunks, project their
cool measure, summon
the helicopter.

The sky pales, a weird ochre.
All yellow, I'm flying an octave
below the shareholders. It's
always the same. I remember
their names. I can't see their faces,
I can't read their folders.

THIRD GRADE

The rules
for young girls:

sit   stare   drop
(don't talk) your eyes
under the table, worn
carpet and the silent legs
of chairs. Make friends
with irony, odor and light.
Invisible things listen well,
revealing fine oddities at
birthday parties and funerals.

Learn to mix paint
from spit and berries, write
your name on the sidewalk
six times with a cigarette butt.
Count insects, dandelions,
years of silence, count bottle tops,
apple seeds—keep them
in your dresser drawer

with panties and soap. Practice
breathing—rhythm begins in the blood.
Acquaint yourself with death's low
whistle, know it better than the rules
of Chinese jump rope. Tomorrow
the sky will crack like a tray
of ice cubes and the clouds
shudder glory, glory.

DISLOCATION LESSON IV

We appeal again
to names what else
can we do in the cherry
juice twilight when the
pineapple express
rides the Pacific
seeking cedar cupolas
translating weather
domes to *aburga*,
snow-shook gales
in Alaska.

Dom whispers
French into a foehn,
air descends
a lee of mountain
tops in the Alps.
Chinook, wind.
Sirocco, wind wrapped
like a shy, sexy dress
hesitating in shadows.

There are only two
kinds of objects
in the world: these
you can break
with your hands
and those you cannot.

Dislocation Lesson II

A toy is a doorway.
A boy is foraging
through rain, muddy
vans in his hands.
Saturnia is boring,
Tokyo threadbare.
A sister thinks citrus
and wonders aloud

why toys have faces,
toys have names.
The violence is,
the violence was
indefinite as blue.

Tommy Bahama shirt, blue.
Linen sham, ocean blue.
Devil-girl figure, demon blue.

I made mistakes.
They are displayed
neat as toys
on the blue credenza.

THE VIRGINS OF CHICAGO (4)

The gold lunette just beyond the glass,
the cord, the snag, my lariat mind.
With soft magazines, we let fly like
magdalenes sweeping the stairs. Cassocks
frame damp faces behind the weather.

Slowly through a permissive sky,
an incident, a scar—stars disarticulate
from mud-spattered sails. The billowing
rings in a cell phone ditty, outfitted,
cheeked, sleeping their clarity. Mediums
slung across beds—daughters, madams,
divas feeling it—the Sapphic elastic.

Precursor to this disarming blue
dawn, red in the bent light of fever-
flower gossip. They wake up walking,
the virgins of Chicago, the rhetoric
in their step says fuck the folio.

THE FOUR HORSEMEN
CAVE TO THE MAYOR'S DEMANDS

Would you rather be beautiful
or cool? it asked, and opened
like a Big Mac waiting for teeth.

The day, the day.

Roof-walking in late winter,
red sweater against the grey bricks.

The little girl next door
plays in the yard. She's
coughing and trying
to cry, like us.

Tugging our micro-minis, vacuuming
in the glorious room. We know
what we knew. Not what
we used to, what we used.

Our electronic devices assure us
we got the skillz to pay the bills.
We're content to be sad, perched
like a glass bee on the tip
of a federal holiday.

Some days, the stone natatorium
down the street seems to hold all
dreams under slowly draining water.

THE VIRGINS OF CHICAGO (5)

Where businessmen like to stand
in their underwear, late-night
kites cascade between the heads
of tourists. Each alone and gentle,
uniquely sad, oh that disappointing
brunch on the esplanade.

Instead, I window the Hyatt.
          In my drawing a woman
stands kabuki-neat, holding
a cell phone, poised in red
on a man-hole cover.

The virgins chant:

"Manhole covers of the world
pink anemones and a pagoda
endlessly above the sewer."

Attention urban planners!

The virgins sit where
no one else sits.

We Make Strange Trades

Stomach for knuckle,
"L" for "P," Nietzsche for night-
blindness for those ten dry minutes
before shadows slide over his
turned away face, initiation rites
for shrimp fried rice, organdy
for origami, leather satchel for
tomorrow's green cellophane.
        We trade without knowing
a Potemkin village for a lemon
lollipop ring, ten years of bricked-in
lightning for one glance out the bathroom
window. We trade in broad daylight
what emerges in darkness.
        I trade my fear of death for fear
of breath and puzzled, I end up with both—
some morning in a classroom
whisper, we'll find out what we got.

III

SLIDE

This is how
it goes
shy stumble
into poppy
red we
glissade past
the one
real thing
rings of light
open gray-
green sky
leaves
a stain
to our topspin
sets loose the torpor
we gently wrap
ourselves around
the occasion
testing our press
of sail this
rapport like
rapeseed oil
slicked down
a canvas of skin
and bark we say
"its not that bad"
"we're sumptuous"
murmur or
murder hard
to say which
a sunbath of codeine
or code swept back

like hair held fast
by a ruby
pin glinting in
the wind a trace
opiate we
could do
worse.

A BREATH CATALOGUE

Allegedly, breath
clocks downward,

edged from gasoline
hovering into jackets, jars.

Knock lower? Make noise?

O pantworthy quests
roaming small
towers, tell us!

Utterance. Vow. Wind.
XXX. Your yellow
zones, allegedly.

Breath.

No Breath Found

no thought no breath no eyes no heart no breath in the bellows
no body beside you no breath of fresh air for manufacturer
phillip inman the day is empty no one needs you seven are
squatters in two different worlds hog's breath is better than
no breath at all and when I beheld lo the sinews and the flesh
came up upon them and the skin covered them above but
there was no breath in them as far as I can see there is little
real justification for what we do here there was no breath
left in him red heart yarn red hot no breath strips provide a
clean mouth feeling on-the-go tao of breath no dog breath
unfortunately no one can really smell their own breath whale
calves do not exhibit bad breath because they have no need
to feed themselves and don't have to dive deeply thanks no it
doesn't hurt to breathe just sore to lay on or touch sneezing
coughing wheezing nose itching no match for breath sorry
breath is not in the dictionary cough? no yes no yes yes
copius sputum? no yes no yes possible pallor? no no yes no no
shortness of breath is difficult labored breathing

MERE

You think malaria makes me delirious?
You think incandescence makes me candid?

Uncertainty makes me horny.
It happened. And it could happen again.

The scene of my selves is a yellow mirror, sinuous as
      middle-aged desire.

You speak to me as incantation,
a ritual recitation, magic effect.

So I lean out the window over the street
shaking like a jimsonweed, prickly coarse.
A large purple head trumpeting (and don't
jump to conclusions) nothing.

No song that goes "dum dee dee dum,"
nothing like that, only the toast
of junkyard love or resalable car parts.

You think birdsong makes me contagious?
You think Mayakovsky makes me scanty
                small or meager?

You'd take lactation over
the quills of makimonos?

    O horizontal, O makimonos.

What are they to me, to this
writing on my body, on my
body these manifestos in skin?

STRATEGIES OF LIP, TACTICS OF LATE

The hour is in a pickle,
      the tigers circle and mingle and wait.
A dendrobium twists in his tired eye
        feeding 'feel' on foliage or verbiage.
I kneel in the wet garage.

O smooth-talkers, o ghosts!
tether this red weather.

Untie the kerchief—a grumble-brain,
mouthed to oaks in a yellow rain.

Raise the sill like a thin, white blouse.

Fling high the surf to a dappled psyche,
a too-public eye.

Will we tune to sleep
      and not to hide?
Foray the costa rica
      for a pensive senorita?

          "all the songs the songs go on go on"

and hips, oh morning, swing
      into dawn—I careen, we stitch
and decline, he finds what he
      finds. The hour lets loose
its tiger-stare

out there—we swindle a star,
stash a world in a word

                    so far—

PAGE. PACT. BUOY. BODY.

I write

    "solo, Oslo"

    "so long, go"

You write

    "let me
    maybe
    the trees
    Byzantine"

You write trails
of a backwards winter

        I write "beach towel"
        I enact "sunscreen"

It begins in anise
and ends in Ashville

        "The crickets are deafening,
        like algae to evening"

Snow-banks or vectors
gleaming blank checks

        I sell my possessions,
        kindling my bed

Laughing, you're laughing
checkers, or chess?

        I can't stand to own
        anything beveled or honed

You think of feeding,
all-day riding

        I write "belong,
        bee sting"

Your feet think for you
recording your grieving

        My face is sunburned
        faded and dying

I write

how shadows?

You write

why leaves?

MY MISTER'S EYES ARE SOMETHING LIKE DIM SUM

Dumplings and invention, Sophia in drag!
   a thin drop-stitch, glycerin gaze, meringue-
a-tang yowl laid down with pagan anger
   and charm. Augustine-tine, autumn drizzle, rag-

weed on a Tuesday morning, two daggers
   drawn against a scratchy throat, one danger
sewn in a coat pocket to mildly harangue
   the dawn, an unpredictable snag.

 But for all this, time is our new parade,
   languor and ginger, a noon-filled room,
      "Aeneas the disco king" on the Jersey shore,

swath of green suede between finger and shade,
   the underpants of eloquence, a smoky boon
                  my quirky paramour—I do—and more.

NIGHTSONGS

1.

swept up   aerial!   spun onto
night pulled open spilling
blue ink, memory, a turtle-shaped stain
or parting lips reveal nothing but breath
on a window, the dialect of desire

2.

You drop
into a painting:

her blue lap, cornflower
lemongrass and cedar

"the book tells you everything
tomorrow, too late"

3.

so far, the ocean never sleeps

the bed turned down is a mouth, a palm leaf

jungle, a concertina, the lure, a swing

the dark fields ring and ring

4.

champagne in singapore where she leans
toward the sand a net of hair, whitefish
jump at dawn into the violet fog everywhere
the sky is fractured bone, fingers like coconut
milk dissolve to the wet green it is all breaking
free hair on his neck an ovation to nothing
his chest a night sky unbuttoned by stars

Raving Stark Mad

The yellow figure moves hooded
through the graveyard. *Belle!* of the ball,

greeting guests in the airy air. Overhead
silver-tongue shifts of sky snag

on craggy cloud-mouths. Basil
and diesel upwind. To unwind, he reads

to the dead from *Car & Driver* magazine,
the horizon bleeds a little, he stops

suddenly to interject "Venus sends her
regards. She won't be joining us."

Recalling pirates, a vague depression.
Pittsburgh in July. Three rivers. Rings,

countless cans of soup, valley of coal
eyes. Evening inclines to bellflowers

and bat's wings. "Damn the Marquis
and his fermented honey."

He raves stark ankles, white
in the green, milking the dead.

"Magical Thinking"

Lying in your bed we shove off, imagine
the task of imagining. A ladder looms

from us, fourteen minutes drop dead
like bees from the patio. Our spangled

this. Still and piled up we are "that"
to the doorway. Our ship totes a tiny

executor reflected in alley-light, a rotating
blossom singed by microwave light.

Everything wide, there's so much time
to make a glockenspiel of wall-paint

and moccasins. How long do steel bars
cradle the play of bells? We hover by

the body of a single note; no dog hair, no
watering can to break our framed resistance.

We drift in to the stinging lull, percussive.

Winter

Open wide your
                    mouth of jade   flame, spill

your freckled gems like salt
                         on a snow-drift
                                    brain.

Slick my lips
with a silver
       pitch
                 that slips, a bird's spiral
                 switch to southern tongues.

I'm a woman's hand
                     holding a papered worm-thin secret.

You,
a stiletto
beam, a meager
spoon, a nap at 3

in the "afterwards"
                 a black-sea spume.

Nascent, sage, gulfs of air

after Levertov

The dancers emerge over the salt flats

     sway "there is a summer"
     say "the rain, it was no dream"

what they know they have in hand, they love
the human room, its basket of apples

     legs clamor between

                 arrivederci

histories waft in, grafted
in the moment to a ray of skin

"into the open well of centuries"
fly bodies cupping wreck and wear

     grasping tufts, a thought

                 fermata

break   upward to feel, green wings flee

heavy slips free, slit and cross-press
what isn't blessed, fresh-running

     "the dream is blood"

surrounded or not
torque   release   plot

the dancer folds suspended
there alone, half-known

MONTHS FROM NOW IN SWEDEN

In the pictures five young hungers

come to a green with loaves
and locks like a threesome.

Band-blonde boys, Bolshoi and toothsome,
wish upon a struggle with a swan.

Whistle or wing, wind or rind—is it girlish
of us to want so much seawater? We foster

the ritual of polished melon, or melon
polish? I've forgotten—let's take that cruise

in the archipelago, corner Lucia
and moonshine to see where we went wrong.

Erik on my sail, I swear a kiss and a fin
will do the trick. You could hold my hand,

comment on pants, fold my brown slippers, sleep.

EKPHRASTIC

—with thanks to Caspar David Friedrich

Monk by the sea
you're small.
A finger of coal
against ten thousand
reversals of sky
sky sky. You're
summoning, maybe,
Blake's Pieta
or crisp paella,
all the king's
horses, round
red-orange women.

Monk by the sea
your daughters
are calling those
sailors bad names.
We come into
the world. We
regret the sky.
Words settle
on us, a torn
saddle of light.

Infestation by Islands

A song intersecting the archipelago
breaks away in parabola-instincts,

clichés tossed starboard at
midnight, with wrist-watches,

cocktail napkins, strands of hair.
In Baltic waters, fervor means

futbol or maypole, blueberry
liquored down a departing

evening gown. Windows rubbed
with kerosene repel spiders

and fruit flies. Her earrings
are silk egg-sacks waiting

to please, to release spiders
into corners, impending

malaise infests the pitch-black
deck. Against the lights

of Stockholm, she imagines a house
webbed in yellow fever, infection

resting against her shoulder.
Syntax in flames, she announces

cloud-cover, the nothing that can't
be collared by land, air or sea.

CARDIO/SKY

And when the reds arrive moving as if toward a name
Or a distant cabana, zero in on a shelter
As a generation glides with ignorance and grace

Cloud-crack around twist to a peak
                                    lie in the sand alone

Blood vessels stretched to shade
Tuning what the sky slips on over itself
A cask spilled out, colorific-in-time

There's no consummation

Waves slap shore wet and wet and wet
There's no consumption, only being
consumed, an imbroglio imbued with reds

We stroke without contact our delicate imbalance
Panama Red, red letter, red meat or stumble upon

Redivivus
Redivivus come back
Come back to life

Ineffable Green Thing, Loved by All

1. Stick it in your mouth.

"What we see we think we see" wakes up and climbs the dunes.
Significant landscape, the burden you bear boasts one significant
      arm.
A significant arm reaches, and returns.
The other waves furiously, transparent in a cold, cold creek.

shrub, shrub, bush   shrub

Mouth the perfect size, pleated red.
Elliptical sands run from our shoulders,
blindness like berries on an outboard motor.
Cloud-gazing, we become entranced by glare and a proper saint
      sighting.

2. Morning in Death Valley.

The on-board robot abandons its post, tired of the race.
Eight tight arms reach for the same thing: the same buttered
        popcorn, the gold-plated
fly carcass, the same sun, the same small vulnerable sun.
You're the nostalgic green toy in the window,
I'm a wet, red jolly rancher stuck on a dry idea:
The image of the full moon.

rattlesnake rattlesnake scattered shrubby growth

We are in a world of phone booths, medusas.
The past pages the horizon, a world of real weather.
Like Atari in a Mojave landfill, we are inevitable and
disproportionate.
                Let's be very predictable, very translatable,
                        meaner, past due.

AUTHOR'S NOTE

In the poem 'And How' on page 41, the quote "like cats coming out of clocks" is borrowed from Jeff Clark, with thanks.